W9-BXF-665

WINTER

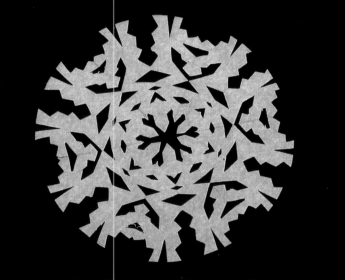

Ruth Thomson

Photography by Peter Millard

FRANKLIN WATTS

LONDON · NEW YORK · SYDNEY · TORONTO

Franklin Watts Inc.
387 Park Avenue South
New York, NY 10016

Library of Congress Cataloging-in-Publication Data

Thomson, Ruth.
Winter / by Ruth Thomson.
p.   cm. — (Starting points)
Includes index.
Summary: Presents a wide variety of projects and activities based on the theme of winter.
ISBN 0-531-10733-7
1. Winter—Juvenile literature.   2. Handicraft—Juvenile literature.
[1. Winter.   2. Handicraft.]   I. Title.   II. Series.
Thomson, Ruth.   Starting points.
QH81. T6115 1989
508—dc20   89-5830   CIP   AC

Editor: Jenny Wood
Design: David Bennett

Typesetting: Typecity
Printed in Belgium

The author and publisher would like to thank Sharon Fuller and Margaret
Howker and children from the Brixton Saturday Explorers' Club (Thomas
Driver, Katie Hunt, Catherine Moore, Laura Riley and Nicholas Sackey) for
their help in the preparation of this book.

Additional photographs:- Biofotos: pages 8 (bottom), 19 (bottom);
Bruce Coleman: pages 7 (top right), 8 (top right and bottom left);
Chris Fairclough Colour Library: page 29;
Natural History Picture Agency: pages 4, 8 (top right), 9 (bottom right), 19 (top left);
Zefa: pages 6, 7 (top left, bottom right and left), 19 (top right).

Poem by Ogden Nash from Parents keep out (J.M. Dent), reprinted by permission of
A.P. Watt on behalf of the Estate of the late Ogden Nash.

CONTENTS

Winter
Is Here

Winter morning

Winter is the king of showmen,
Turning tree stumps into snowmen
And houses into birthday cakes
And spreading sugar over lakes.
Smooth and clean and frosty white,
The world looks good enough to bite.
That's the season to be young,
Catching snowflakes on your tongue.

Snow is snowy when it's snowing,
I'm sorry it's slushy when it's going.

Ogden Nash

Winter Sights

Winter is the season for snow and frost. When the temperature falls to 0°C (32°F) water freezes to ice. In northern countries, lakes and rivers may be frozen for many weeks.

Most broadleaved (deciduous) trees are bare of leaves throughout the winter. You can compare their shapes, and see which direction the branches go and where they divide.

Evergreen trees do not lose their leaves in winter. Many of them have very tough, narrow, shiny leaves which are not damaged by frost and don't break under the weight of snow.

Mistletoe commonly grows on poplar, basswood, willow and hawthorn trees. When the trees are bare, the mistletoe is easy to see. It has sticky white seeds, which birds eat.

Many berries remain on plants all winter, long after the leaves have fallen. They are a nourishing source of food for birds, mice and other animals which are active throughout winter.

In the autumn, farmers plow their fields, leaving rough clods of soil. When the water in the soil freezes and thaws again, the clods break up. The soil becomes crumbly — ideal for sowing seeds in.

Snowdrops appear in woodlands from January. A leaf-like sheath covers the tip of the flowers and protects them as they push their way up through the hard earth and snow.

Animals And Birds

Winter is tough for animals and birds. To keep warm, they need to use more energy than during other seasons, but there is less food available for them.

There are no flying insects around for insect-eaters, nor are there any fresh green shoots for plant-eaters. Many of the small mammals, such as mice, which are food for meat-eaters, die of cold and starvation.

Animals survive winter in different ways. Many birds fly to warmer places, often long distances away. This is called migration.

Other animals, such as chipmunks, bats and bears, find a sheltered place and hibernate. Hibernation is a deep sleep, during which an animal's body temperature drops very low, its muscles stiffen and its heartbeat slows down.

Animals which stay active spend more time in their burrows and may hoard food for freezing days when it is impossible to go foraging.

Many birds rely on berries and seeds for their winter food.

Bats, which feed on insects, eat well during autumn and build up a layer of fat. They find a sheltered place to sleep. The store of fat gives them enough energy to survive the winter.

Foxes are out and about all winter. They depend on their keen senses to find food and grow a thicker coat to keep warm.

Squirrels make a warm winter nest in the fork of a tree. They come out in fine weather to feed on the stores they gathered during the autumn.

Large flocks of Arctic nesting waterbirds migrate south, to places with milder weather, to find food.

Feeding Birds

It is hard for birds to find enough to eat in winter. Put out a food supply for them.

Nuts and cheese

String peanuts and cheese cubes on strong thread using a darning needle. Knot one end of the thread and leave enough length at the other end for tying on to a branch.

Birds don't all eat the same sort of food. Put out a variety of things, such as bones, seeds, bacon rind, raisins, crusts and cereal, to attract different kinds of birds. If you don't have a tree to hang them on, you could make a feeding tepee like this.

Anchor it firmly in the ground, so it doesn't blow over in the wind. Alternatively, make a little twig perch to hang food on.

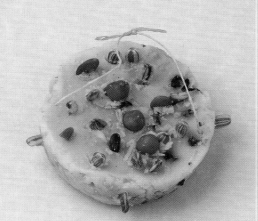

Bird cake

1. Melt some fat or suet in a pan in the oven. Stir in some scraps, such as cooked pasta, rice or potato, raisins and breadcrumbs.
2. Pierce a hole in the base of a plastic pot and thread through a length of string with a large knot on the end.
3. Spoon the mixture into the pot and press it down firmly.
4. Leave it to harden in the refrigerator.

5. Unmold the cake, decorate it with seeds and hang it up.

Bread stars

Fold a slice of thin, white bread corner to corner and cut shapes in it with a pair of scissors. Tie thread to one corner. Bake the bread in a low oven for 15 minutes to harden it.

Winter Buds

When broadleaved trees have no leaves, you can identify them by their winter buds.

In autumn, at the end of the growing season, buds form just above the leaves. When the leaves fall off, the buds, which contain leaves and flowers for the next year, are easy to see. They are covered with thick, overlapping scales or furry hairs to protect them from the cold and from insects.

The buds stay tightly closed until the days begin to lengthen in spring. Sap (water and food) flows up to the buds and swells the tiny leaves inside. The leaves push open the scales and unfold.

The leading bud at the tip of a twig is often larger than the side buds. It contains the main shoot as well as leaves and flowers. It grows more than the other buds.

Each type of tree has buds which are a distinctive size, shape and color, and which are arranged singly, in pairs or in clusters.

A horse chestnut twig

The leading bud. Folded up inside are leaves, flowers and next year's shoot.

The twig grew this much last year.

The leaf buds are arranged in opposite pairs.

This is a girdle scar, left by the scales of last year's leading bud. You can tell the age of a twig by counting its girdle scars.

The horseshoe scar under the bud was left by last year's leaf.

Look at twigs carefully and try drawing them, showing how their buds are arranged.
Notice the differences between these twigs and their buds.

Willow buds are gray and furry and lie close to the twig.
They are closely spaced and are arranged singly.

Ash buds are arranged in pairs on either side
of the twig. They are black and pointed.

Birch buds are arranged alternately.
They often have catkins at the tip.

Sycamore buds are arranged alternately.
They have a girdle scar around them.

Basswood twigs are a zigzag shape
There is a single, reddish-brown bud at each joint.

Stick Creatures

When you go on a winter walk, look for unusual shaped sticks to turn into curious creatures.

Snake

Strip the bark off a wiggly stick and sandpaper it smooth. Glue on a beady eye and a forked twig tongue to make a realistic looking snake.

Old croc

This branch was found already split at one end. Adding paper teeth and a metal pop eye turned it into a very convincing crocodile.

Painted creatures

Some odd-shaped sticks may inspire you to make fantastic imaginary creatures, such as this sea monster.

If you want to paint a stick, brush off any loose pieces and rub it all over with sandpaper. You will probably need several coats of paint to cover the wood completely. If you want the model shiny, brush on a clear coat of varnish once the paint is dry.

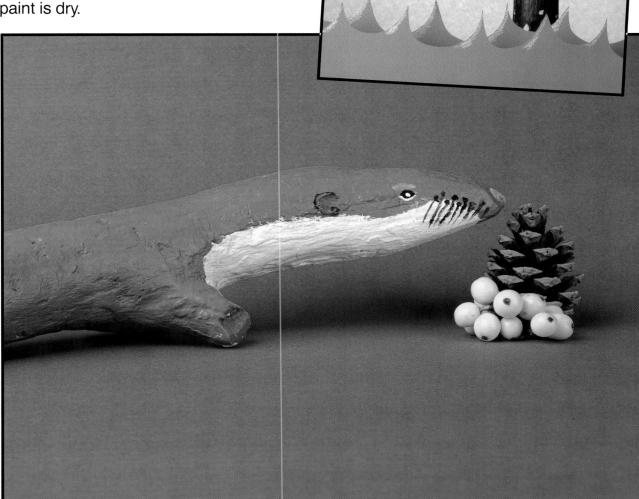

You can add features to your creatures for extra effect. This ermine, for example, has a nose made of modeling clay.

Twig Models

Use sticks, twigs, shoots, dried flowers and stalks to make some models of animals that you can see in winter.

Bird

Make the head and body of a bird by weaving flexible twigs into the right shape. Bind feathers on to some small twigs with cotton to make the wings and tail. Poke the ends of the twigs into the body. Use nutshells or small stones for the eyes and beak.

Fox

For big models like this, it is best to make a skeleton first with some sturdy twigs. Bind them together with ivy or virginia creepers, stripped of leaves. Reinforce the joints with nails if they seem wobbly.

Build up the body by laying straight twigs along the backbone, and tie them in place. Then wrap more flexible twigs around and around the body, poking in the ends.

Make the head separately. Use nuts for the eyes and nose.

Squirrel

Make smaller animals like this by weaving two balls of stems and twigs for the head and body. Attach little bound bundles of twigs for the limbs and ears. Add a sprig of dried flowers for the tail.

Evergreen Trees

Trees which keep their leaves in winter are called evergreens.

Spruce

Holly

Collect some evergreen leaves to see how they look and feel. They are usually dark and tough. They often have a waxy surface, which protects them against wind and prevents them from drying out.

Many evergreen trees are conifers. Conifers are so-called because they bear their seeds in woody cones. Some conifers, such as pines and cedars, have narrow, needle-like leaves, which grow either singly or in bunches. Cypress trees have tiny, overlapping scale-like leaves. Firs and spruces have flat, spiky leaves. Holly is one of the few broadleaved trees that is evergreen.

Cypress

Spruce

Many evergreen trees are triangle-shaped. This helps snow fall off them more easily.

Many conifers grow in a very regular way. In spring, a new shoot grows straight up and branches grow equally on either side. You can tell the age of most conifers by counting each cluster of branches.

Pine

Since evergreen trees always have leaves, they can make food almost all year round. They grow much faster than broadleaved trees, and their trunks grow very straight, so they are widely grown for their timber.

Evergreen Decorations

Collect berries, cones, sprigs of evergreens and bare twigs to make cheap and original Christmas decorations.

Painted evergreens

You can decorate a bunch of holly or ivy by painting on white spots. Hang it up on a colorful ribbon, tied with a big bow.

Advent candles

In some countries, it is a tradition to light an advent candle each Sunday during the month before Christmas.
Make a simple advent candle stand on a cake base or on a circle of card covered with foil. Glue on four candleholders and surround them with sprigs of fir, silver balls, holly and ribbons. A gold painted pine cone looks decorative in the center.

Door wreath

Hang a festive wreath on your front door to welcome visitors. Use a wire, straw or card ring as a base. Bind evergreen sprays all around the ring with soft wire.

Tie on some berries, shiny balls, painted cones and other bright decorations. Make an enormous ribbon bow with long tails to tie on to the bottom of the wreath.

Winter Festivals

Winter celebrations are usually very colorful.

On January 6, many Christians in Spanish speaking countries, celebrate Epiphany. This marks the visit of the Three Wise Men to baby Jesus with their gifts. There are parades through the streets and children receive gifts.

Christmas is the main Christian winter festival. It celebrates the birth of Jesus, in Bethlehem, nearly 2,000 years ago.

New Year is an important winter festival for the Chinese.
Processions of people dressed as lions and dragons perform to music and firecrackers are let off to scare away any evil spirits.

Animal Stencils

Make some enormous stencils of birds and animals and fill them with berries, twigs, seeds or dead leaves.

Making the stencil

Draw a bold, simple outline of an animal on a large sheet of thick paper. Cut it out, remembering to cut from the center of the paper, *not* the outside edge. Reinforce the edges of the stencil with masking tape.

Filling the stencil

Lay the stencil in a sheltered spot, holding it down with sticks, if necessary. Don't remove the stencil until you have completely finished filling it in.

All these stencil animals were made outdoors. If you prefer to make a more permanent picture, lay your stencil over a big piece of card. Glue on seeds, fruits or leaves to fill it.

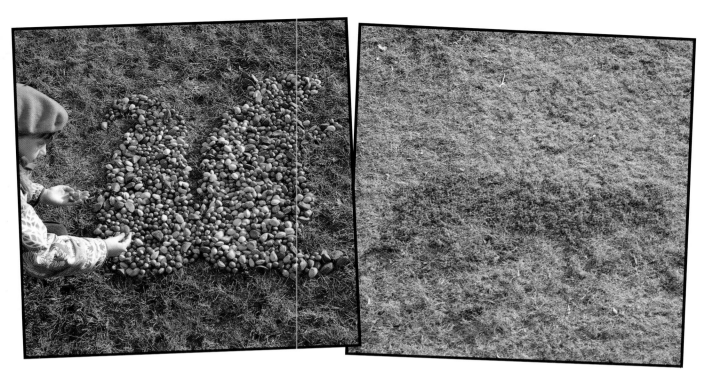

This squirrel was made with hazelnuts.

This fox was made with berries.

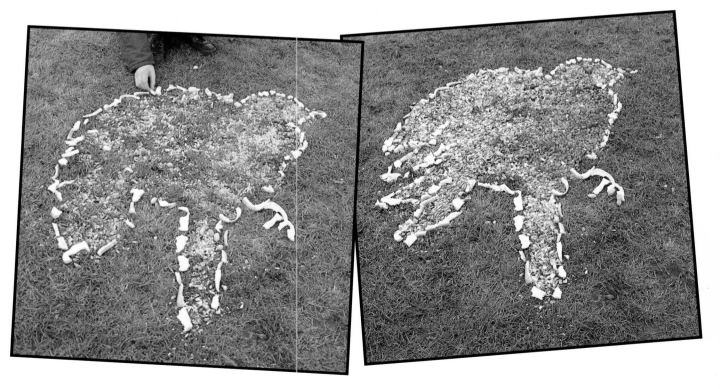

This bird was outlined with bread crusts to give it a definite shape.

It was filled with pumpkin seeds, bird seed and peanuts.

Snowflakes

Paper snowflakes stuck on windows will give your room a festive feeling.

1. Draw around the rim of a cup on to thin paper. Cut the circle out. Fold the circle in half.

2. Now fold the semi-circle into thirds to make this shape. Snip shapes in all the edges.

3. Unfold the paper to see what kind of snowflake you have made.

Winter Tracks

When the ground is wet and muddy or covered with snow, it's a good time to look for animal tracks.

Fox

Dog

A fox track is similar to a dog's, but its trail is straight and almost a single line. When it walks, it puts its hind feet into the prints of its fore feet.

You will find only the tracks of fairly large animals. Small animals, such as mice, voles and weasels, make tunnels under the snow to find food.

You can usually tell what animal has made a track by where you find it. Tracks coming away from a tree, for example, are usually those of a squirrel. Rabbits leave trails near their underground burrow. Tracks on a muddy woodland path will probably be those of deer. Look for fox tracks by the side of hedges or in ditches and hollows.

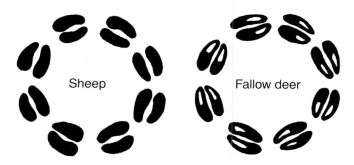

Sheep

Fallow deer

Sheep and deer both have cloven hoofs and their tracks look quite similar, but sheep have one toe bigger than the other. Deer's toes are both the same size.

Rabbit

Hare

Rabbit and hare tracks look rather like exclamation marks. They will be rather blurred, because of their hairy pads.

More Things To Do

Watch buds unfold

Using pruning shears, carefully cut some little twigs from different kinds of trees. Hazel, birch, horse chestnut and willow are the best twigs to choose, because their buds are among the first to come out.

Put them in jars of water and leave them in a sunny place indoors for a week or two. Draw the leaves at different stages as they unfold, and see how many are inside each bud.

Look among the dead leaves

Many small creatures live among the dead leaves under trees and along the hedges. Collect a bagful of leaves to examine at home. Spread them out on a piece of newspaper and see what you discover.

Use a hand lens or a magnifying glass to look at the creatures more closely.

Hare and hounds

This tracking game will warm you up on a cold day and the track can be left to feed hungry birds.

One person or team (the hare) goes out in advance of the others with a large bag of dried bread and 10 painted pebbles.

They drop pieces of bread at intervals to make a trail and hide the pebbles at strategic points along the route.

The second team have to follow the trail and find the pebbles on the way within a given time limit.

Leaf skeletons

Most fallen leaves eventually rot away completely. Sometimes, if you are lucky, you may find a leaf where the soft surface has rotted, but the skeleton, with its veins, is still intact.

Leaf skeletons make pretty decorations for greeting cards. You can make them yourself with fallen leaves or holly leaves. Ask an adult for help with using the stove.

What to do

1. Half fill a saucepan with water. Add a teaspoon of baking powder. Bring the water to the boil and put in the leaves. Simmer until the leafy bits start coming away.
2. After an hour or so, take the pan off the stove and leave the leaves to cool. Gently brush the rest of the soft parts off the skeleton with an old toothbrush or nailbrush. Rinse the skeleton gently under the cold tap.

Twig weaving

Make a weaving with twigs, leaves and colorful berries to use as a Christmas decoration or to put in the garden for birds. If you use it for feeding birds, don't forget to add new food regularly. Once birds are used to you feeding them in a particular spot, they will depend on you providing them with food all winter.

A winter quiz

1. Which of these animals hibernate in winter?
   a) grass snake   b) frog   c) bat
   d) lizard   e) toad   f) bear
   g) chipmunk   h) squirrel

2. At what temperature does water freeze?
   a) 30°C (86°F)   b) 12°C (54°F)
   c) 0°C (32°F)

3. How do birds keep warm in cold weather?
   a) by fluffing up their feathers
   b) by smoothing their feathers
   c) by sitting in their nests

4. How can you work out the age of a twig?
   a) by counting the number of buds on it
   b) by counting the girdle scars
   c) by counting the leaf scars

5. Which of these animals grows a white coat in winter?
   a) a deer b) an Arctic hare c) a squirrel
   d) an ermine e) a field mouse

6. Which of these trees is the odd one out?
   a) holly b) horse chestnut
   c) Scotch pine d) Norway spruce
   e) cypress

Winter words

How would you describe winter? Think about the weather, your surroundings, and feelings.
Here are some useful wintry words to start you thinking.

Weather words
bleak   icicles
frosty   rime
hazy   perishing
icy   drift
chilly
harsh
nip (nippy)
blizzard
raw
windswept
bitter
sleet
slushy
snowy
wintry

Outdoor words
crumbly   scanty
frozen   muddy
fallow   lifeless
clod   shadow
evergreen   slippery
desolate   slithery
hibernate   sleigh
sparkle   camouflage
meager
bare
huddle
resting
burrow
dreary
barren

Indoor words
glow
cheer
blazing
roast
cosy
snug (snuggle)
warm
shelter

Index

Winter quiz answers

1. All the animals, except the squirrel, hibernate in winter.

2. Water freezes at 0°C (32°F).

3. Birds keep warm in cold weather by fluffing up their feathers.

4. You can work out the age of a twig by counting its girdle scars.

5. The Arctic hare and the ermine both grow a white coat in winter.

6. The horse chestnut is the odd one out. It is the only tree which is not evergreen.

PRINTED IN BELGIUM BY
proost
INTERNATIONAL BOOK PRODUCTION